WHAT PEOPLE ARE SAYING ABOUT LABR

'It has been my privil

Mark over the years, his honest counsel during this time. Those of you also lucky enough to have benefited from friendship or mentorship from Mark will recognise his voice in these pages. Everyone else will get an insight into the priceless guidance of one wise man and his equally wise dog.'

Jennie Cronin, Director of People, On the Beach

'Having been lucky enough to preview this book, I felt comforted, inspired, and almost giggled a few times at the perception and insight that the author gave on leadership. It sounded like my friend Mark. Then I realised that he wrote it, and that made perfect sense! Beautifully thoughtful, well written and humble. Read this book. I guarantee you will feel the same way.'

Jo Gilhooley, Chief Marketing Officer, Adarma Security

'Mark epitomises the concept that a good plan well executed far outperforms a great plan poorly executed. Mark turns chaos, activity and entrepreneurial energy into an effective and well organised process, focused on the intended goal. I worked with Mark for close to ten years and was constantly impressed by his calm, his focus, and his clarity of purpose; always keeping his eyes on the goal, maintaining that the right people were assigned to the right roles along the way, and ensuring that the team was connected, motivated, and involved in being part of the solution – no easy task. Mark knows his business. He is a wise guy, an honest guy, and he was certainly instrumental in the control and fluidity of a wildly fast growing entrepreneur-run business.'

Charles Sharland, Serial Entrepreneur, and Investor

'For the last week I have been listening to a book that shares the wisdom of Seneca, Epictetus and Montaigne. I'm glad I took a short break from that to learn from Mark and Meg. Beautifully crafted wisdom bites – I know I'll be dipping back in.'

David Calder, Chief Product Officer, Adarma Security

'Meg is to be congratulated on conveying such wisdom in a way that we mere humans can receive and begin to understand. I've never known a dog with such a gently expressed sense of humour. I begin to smile, laugh even; and then the penny drops!'

Peter Crabtree, Friend, Fellow Traveller and Meg's number one fan!

LABRADOR LEADERSHIP

WISDOM FROM ONE MAN AND HIS DOG

MARK LAWRENCE

LW3 PUBLISHING

Published by LW3 Consulting, The Barn, Dale
Road, Marple SK6 6NL, United Kingdom

LW3 Consulting is a company registered in England, no. 10941361.

www.lw3consulting.com

The Team: Mark Lawrence, Meg,
James Shuttleworth, Emily Shore, Simon Baker

Printed in the United Kingdom
ISBN: 978-1-7390967-0-0

To Alexa, George, Sienna, Quinn, Charlie, Rupert and Dylan who have together bestowed on me my most precious leadership role.

FOREWORD

JIM KENT

I have always felt that ethics in leadership is a fundamental trait. I have been very privileged to have worked with good leaders from whom I have learned most of what I know – I hate to think where I would be if I hadn't had this experience; a principled trial and error if you like. Witnessing leadership from the ground up, I've had my share of success and failure, and both have been amazing teachers. I've been a leader in both small and large businesses and apart from the size and the apparent complexity, navigating to success has always required the same basic beliefs. That first, I have to give people the freedom to act, and secondly, that my success is found in others and not the other way round. How I deal with people sits at the core.

The thoughtful insights into leadership within the following pages therefore strongly resonate with me, and I think the beauty and power of this book is in its reflective simplicity. The topic of leadership is a devilishly complex area, full of jeopardy – especially if approached without thought and care – but this pattern of punchy and thought-provoking observations cuts through to some simple prompts. Success in the leader is often celebrated but failure rarely confronted.

Every reflection in this book is an opportunity for the reader to first ask questions of themselves, and then and only then, of those around them. As a collection, these observations provide new insights and a welcome template. For those who aspire to be good leaders this book offers an opportunity to indulge in their own development, and for established leaders a time to reflect.

Leaders often say that there is no monopoly on wisdom. Yet, if it is derived from experiences which are often painful and costly, then Mark and his dog have opened a door that invites the reader to ask themselves some of the critical questions.

Jim Kent, Summer 2022

Jim has worked in the technology industry for over 40 years, his experience spanning internal leadership in the information technology sector for 20 years and then as CEO/Chairman of several investment backed SMEs, including two in the information technology sector, one in energy technology and two turnarounds. His main focus now is in supporting and guiding boards.

HELLO

Mark and Meg here (I'll let you decide which is which). I am a leadership consultant, Meg is my faithful four-legged friend, and you will mostly find us meandering over hills and dales and hoping we can find our way home again.

As anyone with a Labrador knows, they need a lot of exercise. They need to stretch, explore, and breathe in the great outdoors. It's what keeps them healthy in body and mind. And it turns out that that doesn't just apply to dogs – who knew? I am grateful to Meg for dragging me up and out most days, and for showing me what it looks like to be fully present and ever curious.

I have been developing leaders in a professional capacity for over a decade now, but that means nothing to Meg. So as I pursue my spirited and carefree companion through the countryside, I find myself reflecting afresh on what it looks like to lead and live well. This book is a collection of musings on leadership through the lens of one man, his dog, and a smartphone. Come and join us for a wander...

ON BEING FOLLOWED

When leading, it's a good idea to stop and check that you're actually being followed. If no one is following you then you're not leading – you're just going for a walk.

ON BRIDGES

Bridges are metaphors for trust relationships. They are one of the primary targets during military campaigns because they are vital components of the supply chain that supports advance. The benefits of trust are many. One of the most important is the speed of trust (Covey Jnr): it allows organisations to move much faster. Hence, trust is crucial for high growth organisations.

High growth requires high performance. High performance requires high trust. Lack of trust is one of the reasons larger organisations stop growing and fossilise. Leadership at its best earns trust, fosters trust, and leverages trust to generate speeds of execution that others can only dream about.

ON READING

As Harry S. Truman once said, leaders are readers. If writing is an act of arrogance then reading is an act of humility – an acknowledgement that we have more to learn.

The issue – as Meg so aptly demonstrates – is choice, so choose well! Life is too short to drink bad wine or read bad books. In an age where knowledge is everywhere, I look for the wisdom books. I listen out for the original voice and discard the echoes.

The risk is that we rush to the latest and greatest idea like an amateur football team to the ball. New ideas are valuable. But I prefer to think of them as lenses that challenge my perspective rather than change my position.

My leadership journey has been shaped by some brilliant books. The most significant being Robert Greenleaf's *The Servant Leader*, first published in 1970, which remains (in my opinion) the best book ever written on the subject. Read well, friends.

ON KNOWING YOUR LIMITS

Meg is a gun dog not a sheep dog so, herding sheep? That's definitely not her thing! It's important for leaders to know who they are and what they're good at. This voyage of discovery often involves them bumping into who they are not and what they're not good at. Leaders who think they are good at everything are deceived and dangerous. Leadership at its best looks like the conductor of the orchestra with a baton in their hand, not a one man band with an umbrella strapped to their head and cymbals taped to their knees.

I've had the privilege of working with some brilliant leaders in my career. One of the things they had in common was humility – a confident and accurate assessment of their strengths, and the security and wisdom to delegate away from their weaknesses towards the strengths of others.

Giannis
ALCOHOL
ICE
POPSICLES
Prosecco
& Peach
BELLINI
18+
4.5% ABV

ON HOPE AS FUEL

I've heard it said many a time that hope is not a strategy. I agree in part. But turning that thought on its head: strategy is an expression of hope. The hopeless don't make plans, they make excuses. The hopeful plan precisely because they are full of hope. If strategy is the route map for the journey then hope is the fuel. Without hope, the destination might look amazing but you're going nowhere in a hurry and your strategy will become a holiday brochure for a destination that you never get to see.

ON EMPATHY

Empathy is the hallmark of leadership at its best. I say 'hallmark' not 'capability' because empathy flows from who we are. It's not something we do. Empathy as competency is artificial intelligence: it's inauthentic and painful. Empathy as humanity is emotional intelligence: it's recognising, understanding and – in a healthy way – sharing other people's feelings. Sinek says it can be expressed in three words, 'Is everything OK?' Empathy is the hallmark of those who have learned to recognise, understand and manage their own feelings, and to repackage and repurpose them in the pursuit of helping others.

ON TETHERING TO WISDOM

Meg comes from a lineage of a century of gun dog breeding. She is genetically programmed by nature to run fast and free. But sometimes nurture needs to shape nature, and in this picture that looks like a lead. Leaders have a tendency to rely solely on nature, failing to recognise the importance of tethering themselves to a coach or mentor and giving that person permission to feedback, hold them back, or even stop them in their tracks. Good leaders, like good gun dogs, are products of nurture and nature.

ON VALUES AS TRUE NORTH

Values are the compass of an organisation. Without a compass, we have to rely solely on a map which, by definition, means limiting ourselves to territory that has already been explored. Values empower an organisation to safely explore uncharted territory – to be free to create and innovate, to make its own mark, and not simply to follow in the footsteps of others.

ON FIRST IMPRESSIONS

Waiting to help hang out the washing, Meg? Nope! More like – waiting to steal any pegs that drop from the sky! Things are not always what they appear to be in snapshot. Leadership is the wisdom to know when it's time to question 'face value'. To avoid jumping to the obvious conclusion, inevitably fuelled by confirmation bias. To allow first impressions to be updated by second and third ones. Leadership understands that to assume is sometimes to 'make an ass of u and me'. That snap judgments can sometimes be crap judgments. Lack of due diligence can be costly.

ON PLAYING THE LONG GAME

Meg is a magnificent dog. She is the product of a hundred years of breeding. Her breeder has devoted his life to breeding Labradors. There is no such thing as overnight success. There is no fast forward, there is only forward – one step at a time. Short term success is often a matter of serendipity: a stroke of luck or timing or genius. Long term success is always a matter of strategy: sustained over time by design.

ON THE DANCE OF LEADERSHIP

Some days I'm not sure who is taking who for a walk! 'Who's in charge around here?' is a common but often low-value question. In recent years, leadership has been redefined by the concept of servant leadership, which puts leaders at the bottom not the top. My observation of this is that it still involves hierarchy – albeit inverted. Lately, the concept of leaderless organisations has grown in popularity. This conjures up in me the rather unfortunate image of a headless chicken! I saw one once and, believe me, it wasn't a pretty sight.

Whatever we decide to do with leaders – stick them at the top or the bottom, the back or the front – my view is that we can't afford to bin them altogether. The best metaphor I can come up with is that leadership is like ballroom dancing: when done well, it's hard to tell who's leading and who's following, but at all times there is leadership. And because it's working so well, no one feels the need to ask the question: 'Who's in charge around here?'

ON FACING THE FACTS

Pliny the Elder was wrong – ostriches don't actually bury their heads in the sand. But it turns out that people (and Labradors!) often do, especially when things don't look good or sound good. It's important to understand that you can't deal with what you deny. Don't be afraid of the facts. Sometimes they are friends and sometimes they are foes. When facing them as foes, my best advice is to remember that 'impossible' is a matter of opinion.

ON CLIMBING THE STEPS

We build steps because we understand that it's impossible to reach the top in one go. And yet when it comes to building plans, the executive summary would often be 'run and jump'. When we fail to recognise the power of incremental change we fall short of our goal, not because our mission was impossible but because we made it impossible by not breaking it down into smaller, achievable actions. The journey of a thousand miles doesn't just begin with a single step, it continues and ends with one!

ON PUTTING IN THE PRACTISE

Maxwell describes leadership as influence. This idea can be extrapolated to suggest that since everyone is influencing someone, we are all leaders. I'm not convinced. Leadership may be influence but I don't believe I'm a leader simply because I'm influencing someone.

So what *does* make a leader? Leaders are those who, aware they have influence, have committed themselves to the life long journey of practice – shaping their character and sharpening their skills so that they offer the best version of themselves to those they lead. We can identify them because they lead by example as well as explanation, by inspiring and not just instructing, by showing and not just telling.

ON DISCERNMENT

Leadership is the wisdom to know when it's time to go with the flow and when it's time to swim against the tide. When to harness the momentum of the prevailing currents of popular opinion and conventional wisdom, and when to swim upstream in the face of commonly held views and common sense. Sometimes, leadership is a choice between doing right and being liked. It isn't a popularity contest. That's why political leadership is practically an oxymoron!

ON LISTENING WELL

Much time and energy is invested in training leaders to present. I'm sure the art of public speaking and the science of PowerPoint are important tools in the leaders' kit bag. After all, PowerPoint used badly (which, let's face it, is most of the time), is more like What'sthePoint! But what about the ability to listen? Listening doesn't attract anywhere near the same training budget. Yet those who lead well are those who listen well.

The difference it makes to us when we know we are being listened to is extraordinary. For most of us, being listened to – as opposed to being told what to think or what to do – is so close to being loved that they're almost the same thing. Leaders who listen well generate a level and quality of commitment and motivation in those they lead that cannot be achieved any other way, and all it costs is a few minutes of your time. Not only that, but those who listen are those who learn! Try asking someone, 'What do you think?' And then follow up with, 'That's interesting, tell me more.' Go on...see what happens.

ON RUFFLING FEATHERS

Much has been said about the difference between leaders and managers. I prefer to think about leadership and management as behaviours, rather than leaders and managers as people. Because all leaders need to be able to manage (themselves, if no one else!) and all managers are, in some sense, leaders. There are many ways of distinguishing between leadership and management. I'm going to use these ducks on the Macclesfield canal to help me with mine.

Management tends to spend its time and energy persuading the ducks to line up in a nice, tidy row because it focuses on optimising the status quo. Meanwhile, leadership tends to spend its time and energy sending the ducks flapping for cover because leadership is disruptive – *status quo* is Latin for life and business at the limit of our willingness to take risks. Management pursues efficiency and effectiveness. Leadership pursues vision and venture. It's not a question of good or bad, it's difference. The question is, what's needed in any given situation: is it management or is it leadership?

ON BOUNDARIES

Healthy boundaries are essential for healthy life and leaders. Basically, boundaries exist wherever you end and someone else or something else begins. They're called relationships. Managing our relationships and maintaining these boundaries is vital if we are to live well, love well and lead well. Boundaries exist in many places. Here are some of the most significant:

- You and your core values and beliefs
- You and your husband or wife or partner
- You and your children
- You and your parents
- You and your friends
- You and your boss
- You and the company you work for
- You and those you manage or lead
- You and the investors in your company
- You and the company you have invested in

Breaches in any of these boundaries will take a toll on you mentally, emotionally and physically. So it's wise to regularly walk around the estate of your life and check your boundaries for breaches and, to the extent that it's within your gift to do so, to repair any damage as soon as possible. It's worth remembering that nobody dies wishing they'd spent more time in the office!

ON LETTING GOOD THINGS GROW

Keeping the grass short is a great way to hide the weeds. That's why high control environments look so good. Great leaders don't need to keep the grass short because they rely on culture and not control to do the weeding. Healthy cultures sort the wheat from the chaff without the help of a combine harvester in the form of a fixer who ensures that those who make waves are waved off. Why is this important? Because high control disempowers people and stifles creativity, while a healthy culture empowers them and encourages creativity. The freedom to create – for the many not the few – is messier to manage but equals competitive advantage.

ON STARTING WELL

The answer to the question, 'How do I get from here to there?' is often, 'I wouldn't start from here!' This always makes me smile because it's almost always true! It's as important to know where you are as it is to know where you're going.

A lot of initiatives fail not because we chose the wrong destination but because we were kidding ourselves about our departure point. What we thought was a launch pad turned out to be a lily pad and what we thought was going to be a 100 metre sprint turned out to be a marathon for which we were just not prepared. Locking down the coordinates of the starting point as well as locking in the coordinates of the destination is vitally important for leaders and investors alike.

ON TIMING IT RIGHT

Often, success is about timing. Sometimes the opportunity is real and significant but you just got there a little early. In life and leadership, it's good and heathy to know how to wait and how to wait well (it's called patience); to believe it's only a matter of time (that's called hope); and to hold your position (that's called perseverance).

Freightliner

ON DIFFERENT PATHS

There is usually more than one way to get to where we want to go. Often this is not about right or wrong, it's just difference. But it would be a mistake to focus exclusively on the destination and fail to recognise the importance of the journey.

Seconds after this shot was taken, Meg became very much the centre of attention for a swarm of busy and defensive workers!

ON CHECKING IT OUT

It's said that leaders are more likely to get what they inspect than what they expect. To rely solely on expectation is to risk assumanagement which, as its name suggests, can invite nasty surprises. But it's also wisdom to know who, what, when and how to inspect. To rely solely on inspection is to risk micromanagement, which can invite some equally nasty responses.

ON LEARNING NEW TRICKS

Just a little something to raise a smile! It's important for old dogs to be open to the possibility that new dogs can teach them new tricks – and for new dogs to understand that old dogs actually can learn new tricks. The difference between young and old is not age, it's flexibility. In the process, old dogs also get the opportunity to demonstrate the value of not taking yourself too seriously!

2

ON MOVING THROUGH

This is lock number two. It's one of sixteen. Meg and I walk these most weeks. To walk around them takes the best part of an hour. To navigate through them, the best part of a day. Life and leadership is often punctuated by what feels like a series of locks – situations where we feel restricted and constrained. Locks teach us that navigating through our constraints well is key to helping us get to the next level: to go higher or to go deeper.

When faced with a lock, the temptation is to spend time and energy looking for a work around instead of focussing on the walk through. Growth and success achieved through short circuits is almost always as short lived as the short cut.

ON MEETING FELLOW TRAVELLERS

Sometimes on your leadership journey you come across people who don't look like you or sound like you. It's wisdom to understand that there is strength in diversity and to invest time in building relationships that make the difference make a difference.

ON STANCES

In life and leadership, we are not always responsible for our circumstances but we are always responsible for our 'in-stances'. Leadership is responding, not reacting. Allowing our internal world to shape us. Refusing to allow our external world to bend us out of shape.

Even on a good day I cannot and should not try to control others. But on a good day, and especially on a bad day, I definitely can and should manage myself. Those who would seek to lead the many must first learn to lead the one, and then learn how not to live in reaction to the few.

ON PLAY

It's said that we don't stop playing because we grow old, we grow old because we stop playing. This is as true for organisations as it is for individuals. It's almost universally the case that as organisations get bigger and older they stop having fun. In contrast, almost the only thing that's mandatory at a start-up is play. Why? Because they recognise that having fun is good for us, individually and organisationally.

Play increases motivation, innovation and team work. It improves our mental, emotional and physical health. Having fun recognises that, fundamentally, we all continue to come to work because we enjoy ourselves. If we don't play, most likely we won't stay. Or – even worse – we do stay and we show up as present but not productive.

ON KEEPING IT SIMPLE

Sometimes, in life and leadership, we find ourselves unable to see the woods for the trees. We lose ourselves and sight of the big picture in a forest of detail. There is a tendency in all of us to over complicate things. The power of simplicity is hard to overstate. Organisations, especially IT organisations, often find themselves wallowing in complexity, invariably of their own making. This impacts customer experience and profitability. Leadership often looks like obsessive focus on simplicity and sounds like a chainsaw!

ON SHADOWING

The concept of shadowing as a means of learning is well understood but less well practised – particularly in the area of leadership. There are hundreds of leadership courses and thousands of leadership books but there is a limit to how much you can learn from the PowerPoint presentation and the printed page. None of these are substitutes for what Maxwell calls the 'evaluated experience' gained by those who have led (and bled!) in the real world.

That experience is not theory cooked up in the leadership laboratory, it's wisdom forged in the furnace of failure and celebrated on the summit of success. Shadowing provides a priceless opportunity to see experience at work in the real world, in real time. Wherever you are on your leadership journey there is almost certainly the opportunity to shadow and be shadowed. Seize it.

ON STRADDLING DITCHES

In life and leadership, we're encouraged to stay on the straight and narrow, avoiding the ditches of extreme on either side of the road. I recently participated in a personality test in which empathy and tough mindedness were placed on opposite sides of a spectrum. The result declared me to be highly empathic and, by implication, weak minded. Needless to say this test bothered me! It wasn't just the result but the assumption that it's not possible to be empathic AND tough minded – that they are mutually exclusive attributes.

Those who know me well know that I am an avid proponent of 'BOTH...AND!' It's entirely possible to be empathic and tough minded. Whenever you're tempted to put two things on opposite sides of a spectrum, run the mutual exclusivity test and ask yourself: can 'both...and' apply? If so, then the spectrum is bunkum.

As an aside: high empathy and tough mindedness in a leader is a powerful combination. It means that not only will you do the right thing, but you will have the courage to do it the right way precisely because you care. (In my experience, tough minded doesn't always equal brave!) You will care about the journey and people will follow you for the right reasons – through the good, the bad and the ugly.

ON ROOTS AND FRUIT

What exists within leaders in seed form takes root and bears fruit in the organisations they lead. An organisation becomes a magnifying mirror of the best and worst of its leaders. If you don't believe me, check out the dress code of the leader and their followers. That's why leaders should pay attention to what's growing in their own lives, and not just the organisations they lead, and why they must lead as team – to offer a range of wardrobe options if nothing else! The personal transformation of its leaders is a prerequisite, a catalyst and a constraint to the health and growth of an organisation.

ON WALKING AND TALKING

A busy and brilliant week finishes with us sitting on a log in the woods, reflecting on the power of talking. Although Meg seems to prefer power walking, we've agreed – perhaps unsurprisingly – that most problems can be solved by a good walk and a good talk. Both, and!

What Meg is actually thinking here:
'Is he going to give me any of his
sandwiches?'

ON TAKING A MOMENT

This is Meg in one of her more thoughtful moments. As a working Labrador she doesn't have all that many! Almost everything she does is instinct. As leaders, we are often under pressure to make decisions and make them quickly. 'Let me think about that' is regularly interpreted as a sign of weakness. And yet we know that quality is often a function of time – think cheese and wine!

Reflection offers us the opportunity to check our understanding, temper logic with emotion, and bring the heat of the moment into the cold light of day. A reflected decision may take longer but it might also last longer.

ON PERSPECTIVE

It's important to be able to distinguish between truth and perspective: those things which are absolutes, that don't change no matter what angle you look at them from, contrasted with those things that look different if you look at them differently.

As a leader, it's vital to be able to see things from different mountain tops, to see things through the other person's eyes, to see what they see and acknowledge that some things are a matter of perspective – not right or wrong. The remarkable thing is that, so often, if we change the way we look at things, the things we look at change.

ON BENCHMARKING

If success is the destination then the journey is often characterised by benchmarking. The idea that you compare yourself to those who are better than you and take action to improve. The goal is to be better and, often, to be different to the rest of the pack.

Whenever I find myself involved in these conversations I always think, and almost always suggest, that the pursuit to be better than the rest and different to the rest should never overtake the need to remain authentic. Authenticity assures quality and is a more powerful marketing strategy than being different. It seems to me that Meg knows who she is and has no intention of being anyone or anything else.

ON THE ROCKS

As a leader, you can often find yourself between a rock and a hard place – surrounded by questions to which it seems there are no perfect answers. That may be true, but some answers are better than others. Leadership is about making the right decisions for the right reasons. This doesn't solve all of your problems. It creates the right ones.

ACKNOWLEDGEMENTS

This book reflects some of my greatest passions – Labradors and leadership, walking and talking. It's the first fruits of years of learning and the product of relentless encouragement. To my family, friends, and fellow travellers who have championed me and challenged me not just to talk a good story but to write a good book – or maybe more than one! To those I have had the privilege to lead, and to those I have had the privilege to be led by. I have learned so much from all of you – much of it captured in this book. I suspect you might even recognise yourselves along the way. To Jeremy from Fenway Labradors, who has been breeding working Labradors for over 50 years. Thank you for trusting us with one of your own, Fenway Rosa (aka Meg). To Ian and Liz from Lower Dale Farm Equestrian Centre, who kindly allow Meg and me to walk the land so much that I'm pretty sure Meg thinks it's hers. To Andy from Storyhouse Creatives, who instilled the courage and provided the creativity that helped me bring LW3 to life. To Simon from Thirteen Creative and Emily from Selwyn Shore, whose creative gifts have helped transform a few photographs and notes into this beautiful book. To Jim for his belief in me and his willingness to contribute to this project. Quoting Jim, as I have done many times over the years, he is 'one of those good leaders from whom I have learned most of what I know.' And finally, to my wife Sarah, who has – more than any other – shown me what it is to live well, love well and lead well, and who every day encourages me to do the same. Everyone, and everything, is grace.

LW3 Consulting: Live Well, Love Well, Lead Well

Mark is the founder and director of LW3, a consultancy business established on the foundation of his own leadership journey.

LW3 works with teams and individuals to help them succeed in a meaningful and sustainable way; encouraging organisations to grow up without growing old.

If you would like to find out more about Mark and LW3, please visit www.lw3consulting.com